Sid

Written by Diana Noonan
Illustrated by Keith Olsen

PEARSON

Sid Sneaky's last name wasn't 'Sneaky' for nothing. He was **as slippery as a snake**. He was **as cunning as a fox**. But the day he met Lolla the cow, Sid's luck ran out.

Sid was driving past Daisybank Farm when he spotted Lolla. Right away he noticed the special pattern on her side. It was a black blob. But not just any black blob. It was a black blob in the shape of America.

"I must have that cow!" squealed Sid. "I'll show her to the world. She'll make me a millionaire!" He stopped the car.

"I'll give you three hundred dollars for your cow," Sid told Farmer Fred. Three hundred dollars was a lot for a cow.

"It's a deal!" said Farmer Fred. "But only if Lolla agrees."

Lolla was tired of eating grass. She was bored with the same old view. She was fed up with being like every other cow. When Sid promised Lolla **fame and fortune**, she couldn't wait to go with him.

But right from the start, things were not as good as Sid had promised.

Lolla's 'caravan' was a dark horse trailer. Her bed was the floor of the trailer. Sid didn't take much notice of Lolla. He didn't talk to her. He didn't brush her. He didn't feed her.

Wherever Sid stopped to show off Lolla, he sold food. There was candy floss and popcorn. There were cupcakes and French fries. While Sid took the money, Lolla ate the leftovers. She loved them.

For a while, things were okay. But after a few weeks, Lolla wanted a break. She was tired of riding in her dark trailer. She was tired of smiling for cameras. She'd had enough of people poking her map of America. Lolla wanted some peace and quiet.

"What!" roared Sid when Lolla told him. "No way. You're mine! I paid three hundred dollars for you. You're making money, honey, and that's the way it will stay."

Lolla was very sad. She missed her friends. She missed her fresh, green grass. She missed Farmer Fred and Daisybank Farm. She grew very, very homesick. But Sid Sneaky didn't care.

"Smile for the cameras!" Sid hissed at Lolla. But Lolla was too sad to smile. "Turn around so everyone can see your map of America," he ordered. But Lolla was too homesick to move.

Sid Sneaky grew very cross. The more he growled, the sadder Lolla felt. And the sadder Lolla felt, the more she ate. She ate more candyfloss and popcorn. She ate more and more French fries. She ate twenty cupcakes a day! Lolla grew **fatter** and **fatter**. And then, one day, something about Lolla began to change.

"That's not a map of America!" said a man, pointing at Lolla. "That's a ... a..."

"That's just a **black blob**!" said a boy.

"Yes, it's just a **blob**," everyone began shouting. "We want our money back!"

It was true. Lolla had grown so fat that she'd stretched the map right out of shape.

Sid Sneaky was furious! "That's it!" he shouted at Lolla. "You're useless. You're no good to anyone. I'm taking you back to where I got you!"

Lolla couldn't believe her ears. She was so happy. She skipped into her trailer with a big smile on her face.

When Sid Sneaky drove into the yard at Daisybank Farm, Farmer Fred looked very surprised.

"Here's your cow!" shouted Sid. "She's nothing but a fake! Look, there's no map of America on the side of this cow. There's just a big, black blob. I want my money back!"

"There was a map of America there last time I looked," said Farmer Fred. "You must have done something to it. I'm not taking Lolla back unless you pay me."

Sid Sneaky hopped up and down. He was furious. **"But I can't show her any more!"** he shouted.

Lolla licked her lips and wandered over to her field. She took a big bite of grass. It was delicious! She took a big drink of fresh water. **Mmm-mm**! It tasted so good.

Farmer Fred watched Lolla take another bite of grass. "It's going to cost you a lot of money to feed her," he said to Sid.

Sid Sneaky looked as if he might explode with fury. "All right! All right!" he screeched. "I'll give you a hundred dollars to take her back."

"Three hundred," said Farmer Fred. "I won't take a cent less."

Sid Sneaky took out his wad of money. He paid Farmer Fred and stormed off.

A few months later, Lolla was looking like her old self. The black blob on her side looked just like a map of America.

Farmer Fred nailed Sid's sign to the gate. Then he painted two extra words onto it. They said, '**Saturdays only**'.

Lolla was happy to work one day a week. It helped Farmer Fred, and it made her feel special. "I'm famous," she smiled, "but not too famous!"

Sid Sneaky is a Narrative.

A **narrative** has an **introduction**. It tells ...

- **who** the story is about (the characters)
- **where** the story happened
- **when** the story happened.

Introduction	
Who	
Where	
When	The day Sid Sneaky met Lolla the cow.

A narrative has a **problem** and a **solution**.

Problem

Solution

Guide Notes

Title: Sid Sneaky
Stage: Fluency
Text Form: Narrative
Approach: Guided Reading
Processes: Thinking Critically, Exploring Language, Processing Information
Written and Visual Focus: Illustrative Text

THINKING CRITICALLY
(sample questions)
- What do you think the author meant when she said "Sid Sneaky's last name wasn't 'Sneaky' for nothing"?
- Why do you think the author described Sid Sneaky as being "as slippery as a snake"?
- Look at pages 6-7. How do you think the author wants you to feel about the way Sid Sneaky treats Lolla?
- Look at pages 8-9. What is your opinion of Sid Sneaky? How would you describe him?
- Look at pages 10-11. Do you think it was fair of the people to want their money back? Why or why not?
- Look at pages 12-13. What do you think Sid meant when he said Lolla was "nothing but a fake"?
- Look at pages 14-15. Do you think it was fair of Farmer Fred to ask for his three hundred dollars? Why or why not?
- Why do you think the author wrote this story?

EXPLORING LANGUAGE

Terminology
Spread, author and illustrator credits, imprint information, ISBN number

Vocabulary
Clarify: cunning, millionaire, deal, fame, fortune, homesick, explode with fury, wad of money, stormed off
Adjectives: *special* pattern, *fresh green* grass, *same old* view, *dark* horse trailer
Pronouns: he, it, me, we, she, him, her
Simile: as slippery as a snake, as cunning as a fox
Alliteration: Sid Sneaky, slippery as a snake
Focus the students' attention on **homonyms, antonyms** and **synonyms** if appropriate.

Print Conventions
Exclamation marks, apostrophes – possessive (Lolla's), contraction (she'll, didn't, we'll, there's, couldn't)